W9-CCD-278

POCKET GUIDE TO

TURTLES, SNAKES AND, OTHER REPTILES

Lincoln
Children's Books

WELCOME TO THIS BOOK!

In this book, you will learn all about the wonderful world of reptiles. Here's how to navigate the pages.

Six chapter headers introduce you to the reptile groups.

CROCODILIANS

Crocodilians are cousins of dinosaurs and the closest living relatives of birds. They live in tropical and subtropical areas and spend most of their time in water, but breathe air. All 23 species have a long body, short legs, a tail flattened from side to side, and skin armored with bony plates. Their powerful jaws and pointed teeth make all crocodilians incredible predators.

Here are the crocodilians! In this group are crocodiles, alligators, caimans, and gharials.

Family and species spreads let you go into more depth. Not every species or family is listed in this book, as there are too many to fit. This selection should give you an idea of the wide variety of reptile life on Earth.

Group name

Family name

Number of species in that group

Example species

Learn more about this species in "A Closer Look"

"Did You Know?" boxes give more information on the species and the group

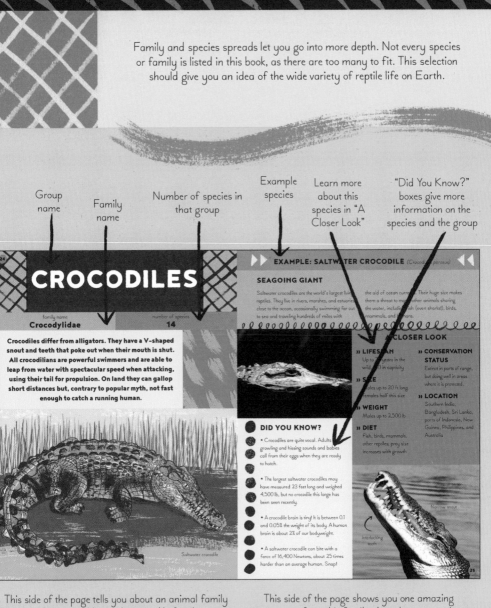

CROCODILES

family name
Crocodylidae

number of species
14

Crocodiles differ from alligators. They have a V-shaped snout and teeth that poke out when their mouth is shut. All crocodilians are powerful swimmers and are able to leap from water with spectacular speed when attacking, using their tail for propulsion. On land they can gallop short distances but, contrary to popular myth, not fast enough to catch a running human.

EXAMPLE: SALTWATER CROCODILE (*Crocodylus porosus*)

SEAGOING GIANT

Saltwater crocodiles are the world's largest living reptiles. They live in rivers, marshes, and estuaries close to the ocean, occasionally swimming far out to sea and traveling hundreds of miles with the aid of ocean currents. Their huge size makes them a threat to most other animals sharing the water, including fish (even sharks), birds, mammals, and humans.

A CLOSER LOOK

» **LIFESPAN**
Up to __ years in the wild, __ in captivity

» **SIZE**
Males up to 20 ft long, females half their size

» **WEIGHT**
Males up to 2,500 lb

» **DIET**
Fish, birds, mammals, other reptiles; prey size increases with growth

» **CONSERVATION STATUS**
Extinct in parts of range, but doing well in areas where it is protected.

» **LOCATION**
Southern India, Bangladesh, Sri Lanka, parts of Indonesia, New Guinea, Philippines, and Australia

DID YOU KNOW?

• Crocodiles are quite vocal. Adults growling and hissing sounds and babies call from their eggs when they are ready to hatch.

• The largest saltwater crocodiles may have measured 23 feet long and weighed 4,500 lb, but no crocodile this large has been seen recently.

• A crocodile brain is tiny. It is between 0.1 and 0.05% the weight of its body. A human brain is about 2% of our bodyweight.

• A saltwater crocodile can bite with a force of 16,400 Newtons, about 25 times harder than an average human. Snap!

Saltwater crocodile

Narrow snout

interlocking teeth

This side of the page tells you about an animal family in this group. Here is the crocodile family.

This side of the page shows you one amazing creature from this family: the saltwater croc!

LIFE ON EARTH

Life on Earth is amazingly diverse. Scientists have named nearly two million different species, with millions more still to be discovered. A species is a group of plants, animals, fungi, or microorganisms that look similar and are able to breed with each other. There are far too many species for anyone to know them all, but we can usually figure out what group an organism belongs to by looking for shared characteristics such as feathery wings in birds, six legs in insects, and warm, furry bodies and milk glands in mammals.

The way a species looks and behaves is influenced by its genes. Like the computer code controlling the apps that run a machine, genes carry instructions for building and operating a living thing, and there is a copy of the code in every cell of a body. Closely related animals have similar genetic codes. These codes can be read by scientists, but it's usually easier to look at the animal or plant and compare it with others to see where it fits in the grand scheme of life.

NAMING NAMES

All life-forms can be classified into kingdoms. Within a kingdom, every known species is given a unique scientific name, which is the same in all languages. Scientific names have two parts. The first part tells you which small group or genus of similar organisms it belongs to, such as *Crocodylus* for crocodiles. The second part of the name is used only for that particular species, for example *Crocodylus porosus* for the saltwater crocodile. The chart on the right shows how to classify this species, putting it into smaller and smaller groups until you get just one species.

KINGDOM: ANIMALIA
This kingdom includes all animals.

PHYLUM: CHORDATA
This includes all animals that have a backbone.

CLASS: REPTILIA
Scaly air-breathing animals descended from four-legged ancestors.

ORDER: Crocodilia
Armored semi-aquatic predatory reptiles with long, powerful jaws.

FAMILY: Crocodylidae
A group of closey related crocodilians, commonly known as crocodiles.

GENUS: *Crocodylus*
Closely related species of crocodiles.

SPECIES: *Crocodylus porosus*
The saltwater crocodile, a unit of life that is able to reproduce with others of its kind.

Saltwater crocodile!

ANIMAL GROUPS

In the grand tree of life, reptiles sit on the same big branch as fish, amphibians, birds, and mammals. These are all the animals with backbones, and they are known as chordates or vertebrates.

FISH have gills and fins and live in water. They have skeletons made from bone or cartilage.

Most AMPHIBIANS spend some of their life breathing air, but their unshelled eggs develop in water.

BIRDS are feathered and warm-blooded and lay chalky-shelled eggs.

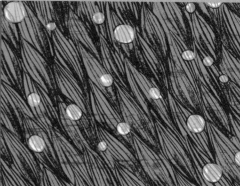

MAMMALS are warm-blooded and feed their young milk. Most are furry and give birth to live young.

REPTILE GROUPS

Several reptile groups have gone extinct. They include the flying pterosaurs, the sea-going ichthyosaurs and plesiosaurs, and most of the greatest group of all—the dinosaurs. Dinosaurs ruled the Earth for more than 140 million years, up until 66 million years ago, when nearly all of them went extinct. But not quite all...The survivors were a special group, set apart by their feathered wings and powered flight. Those last dinosaurs are still with us now, but we call them birds.

The remaining reptiles belong to four groups, the turtles and tortoises (testudines); the crocodiles and alligators (crocodilians); the snakes, lizards, and worm lizards (squamates); and the tuataras (rhynchocephalians).

Testudines

Squamates

Crocodilians

Rhynchocephalians

WHAT IS A REPTILE?

Reptiles are air-breathing vertebrates (animals with backbones). Like amphibians, birds and mammals, reptiles are *tetrapods*, from *tetra* meaning "four" and *pod* for "leg." This is because all these groups evolved from a four-legged air-breathing ancestor, even though some have since lost legs–like snakes.

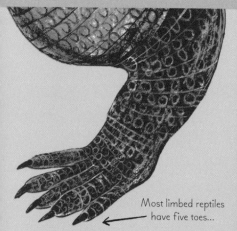

Most limbed reptiles have five toes...

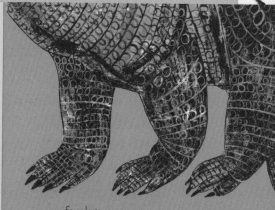

four legs...

and a tail.

IDENTIFYING REPTILES

All reptiles are covered in scales made from the same substance as mammal hair, claws, and bird feathers—a protein called keratin.
Like most animals, reptiles shed their skin now and then to allow growth and to replace worn or damaged surfaces. In most groups, the skin is molted gradually or in patches, but snakes usually cast it off all at once. Scales can be bead-like, smooth, or keeled.

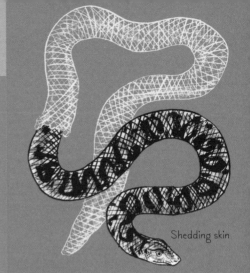
Shedding skin

SCALES

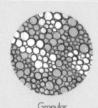
Granular

Smooth

Keeled

Sunbathing

Unlike birds and mammals, the body temperature of reptiles changes depending on their surroundings. They often sunbathe to warm up, and seek shade or water to cool down. Scientists call them ectothermic rather than cold-blooded because a reptile in a hot place can actually be very warm.

PUPILS

Horizontal

Round

Vertical

REPTILE LIFE

Reptiles eat a very wide variety of foods, from algae and land plants to large and small animal prey and carrion (dead animals). Some are very specialized feeders–the leatherback turtle eats almost nothing but jellyfish, while others devour almost anything that can fit into their mouth.

Leatherback turtle

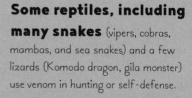

Fangs

Some reptiles, including many snakes (vipers, cobras, mambas, and sea snakes) and a few lizards (Komodo dragon, gila monster) use venom in hunting or self-defense.

Inland taipan

The most potent venom is thought to belong to the inland taipan–the venom in one bite from this infamous Australian snake could kill 100 people.

REPTILE BABIES

Reptiles reproduce by laying eggs or giving birth to live young. The eggs have leathery or chalky shells, and are usually hidden in soil or under wood or stones.

Eggs

Hatchlings

In many species, the temperature of the nest affects whether the eggs hatch into males or females.

Young Komodo dragon

In a few species of lizard, including the Komodo dragon, females sometimes lay eggs without mating. The hatchlings are exact copies, or clones, of their mother.

TURTLES &

TORTOISES

Turtles first appeared on Earth about 160 million years ago. But fossils of turtle-like relatives extend back more than 220 million years, so they shared much of their history with the dinosaurs. All have a shell to protect their body, and many can pull their head and limbs inside it. Aquatic species have flippers instead of feet. The smallest tortoise, the South African speckled tortoise, can rest in the palm of your hand. The largest turtle, the leatherback turtle, is up to 7 feet long.

SEA TURTLES

infraorder name	number of species
Chelonioidea	**7**

Sea turtles are the largest and most water-loving turtles and spend nearly their whole lives at sea. They are powerful swimmers, thanks to their paddle-shaped flippers, but find moving on land difficult. They live in warm seas around the world and swim up to 12,000 miles a year between feeding and breeding places. Only female sea turtles ever come ashore as adults, in order to lay their eggs.

Green turtle

OCEAN WANDERER

This handsome green turtle is found in warm oceans around the world. Green turtles may travel 5,000 miles a year in search of food, but adults return to the same breeding area every year. The species is listed as endangered due to hunting and habitat loss.

Sharp beak

A CLOSER LOOK

» **LIFESPAN**
80-100 years

» **SIZE**
2.5-3.5 ft long, with a shell the size of a trash can lid

» **WEIGHT**
150-400 lb

» **DIET**
Jellyfish, shrimp, mollusks, and algae

» **CONSERVATION STATUS**
Endangered. About 90,000 nesting females in the world

» **LOCATION**
Tropical and subtropical waters of the Pacific, Atlantic, and Indian Oceans and adjoining seas

DID YOU KNOW?

★ Sea turtles are able to drink seawater thanks to special glands that help their body get rid of salt.

★ Most sea turtles surface roughly every five minutes to breathe.

★ Sea turtles sometimes doze at the surface but can also sleep underwater, holding their breath for hours.

★ Female sea turtles visit the same breeding beach every year to bury hundreds of eggs in the sand. Then they return to the sea and never see their babies hatch.

Hatchling

Paddle-like flippers

POND & RIVER TURTLES

family name	number of species
Emydidae	**93-95**

This group includes turtles and terrapins of many shapes and sizes. Some have a domed or knobbly shell, while others are flat. The smallest are less than 5 inches long, and the largest are about 2 feet long. Most live in freshwater, but some terrapins are land dwellers. Many feed on smaller animals such as fish, shrimp, and worms, but several species become vegetarian as they grow up.

Red-eared terrapin

THE GREAT INVADER

The red-eared terrapin is also known as the red-eared slider because of its habit of sunbathing on banks and floating logs and slipping back into the water when disturbed. It is named for the scarlet flashes on the sides of its head. The species is often kept as a pet and is easy to look after.

Tucked inside its shell

A CLOSER LOOK

» LIFESPAN
Usually 20-30 years

» SIZE
3.5-12 in long, some grow to 16 in

» WEIGHT
0.5-6.5 lb

» DIET
Adults are plant-eaters; young turtles eat almost anything they can swallow

» CONSERVATION STATUS
Not threatened, introduced and highly invasive outside native range

» LOCATION
Native to southern USA and Mexico, but unwanted pets have invaded watery habitats on all continents except Antarctica

DID YOU KNOW?

* Even a hard-shelled adult turtle can be killed by the powerful bite of an alligator or a jaguar.

* Many species of turtle are facing extinction because too many are taken from the wild to be sold as pets.

* Many freshwater turtles spend the winter underwater, hibernating for up to six months without needing to breathe air.

* In softshell turtles the carapace is tough but bendy, like leather. It is lighter than a bone shell, allowing the turtles to move with surprising speed and agility.

Red marking

SNAPPING TURTLES

family name	number of species
Chelydridae	**6**

Snapping turtles are meat-eaters, armed with powerful jaws and a hooked beak, which is perfect for trapping, stabbing, and crushing their prey. They are usually found in water, but travel long distances over land in search of new homes or nest sites. Common snapping turtles cope well with the cold, and have been known to remain active under the ice of frozen ponds.

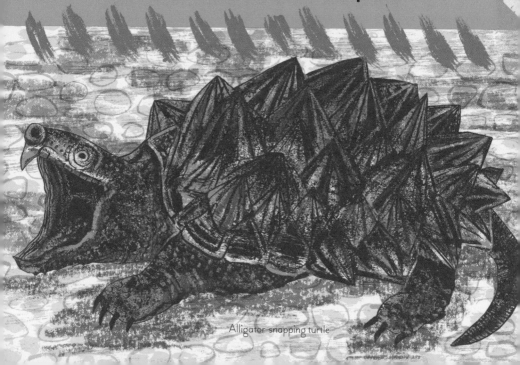

Alligator snapping turtle

EXAMPLE: ALLIGATOR SNAPPING TURTLE *(Macrochelys temmincki)*

A MIGHTY SNEAKY BITE

The alligator snapping turtle is one of the largest freshwater turtles. The muscular jaws and fearsome beak could easily bite off your fingers, but they do not attack humans without good reason. The shell is heavy, with three rows of bony knobbles giving it an alligator-like appearance when glimpsed in murky water. Its body is camouflaged and it hunts by ambush, luring prey such as small fish closer with a worm-like scrap of pink flesh near the tip of its tongue.

A CLOSER LOOK

» LIFESPAN
Over 100 years, possibly up to 200 years

» SIZE
Up to 30 in long

» WEIGHT
Up to 220 lb, occasionally more

» DIET
Fish, clams, crustaceans, snakes, frogs, other turtles, and even mammals; also feeds on dead animals

» CONSERVATION STATUS
Vulnerable, and in need of protection

» LOCATION
Freshwater in southeastern USA

DID YOU KNOW?

* Snapping turtles are still hunted in some parts of the USA and used to make tinned soup.

* Snapping turtles add to their camouflage by allowing algae to grow on their shell and scales.

* The long neck of a common snapping turtle allows it to reach around and bite anyone picking it up!

* Snapping turtles continue to grow for as long as they live. The plates of their shells develop rings, like those in a tree trunk, which reveal their age in years.

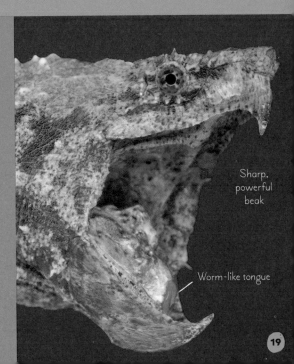

Sharp, powerful beak

Worm-like tongue

TORTOISES

family name	number of species
Testudinidae	**40–50**

Tortoises live on land and eat plant material such as grasses, leaves, and fruits. They are usually active by day, but avoid heat by resting in shade. In areas with cooler winters, they seek a secure hiding place such as a burrow or rock crevice in which to hibernate. Tortoises are famously slow moving, and giant tortoises travel at less than 0.18 miles an hour, but the much smaller leopard tortoise can sprint more than three times as fast over short distances.

Galápagos giant tortoise

GENTLE GIANTS

The tortoises of the remote Galápagos Islands are the largest in the world. Charles Darwin noticed differences in the tortoises between each island.

In some the shell is a dome, in others the front rises in a saddle shape, allowing the animal to reach up to feed on shrubs. Scientists disagree on whether to treat them as one species or several different ones.

A CLOSER LOOK

» LIFESPAN
Up to 170 years

» SIZE
Up to 6 ft long

» WEIGHT
Up to 900 lb

» DIET
Wholly vegetarian, and most of its water comes from food

» CONSERVATION STATUS
The total population is about 19,000 and is slowly increasing thanks to conservation

» LOCATION
Galápagos Islands

DID YOU KNOW?

★ Galápago is Spanish for "tortoise." So the Galápagos Islands are named after their tortoises, and Galápagos tortoises are named after the islands!

★ The Pinta Island giant tortoise went extinct in 2012 when the last one, a 102-year-old male named Lonesome George, died.

★ Giant tortoises are among the longest living animals. A Seychelles giant tortoise named Jonathan living on the island of St. Helena is thought to be at least 180 years old.

★ Giant tortoises can swim surprisingly well–it is thought that they first reached remote islands by drifting on ocean currents.

CROCODILIANS

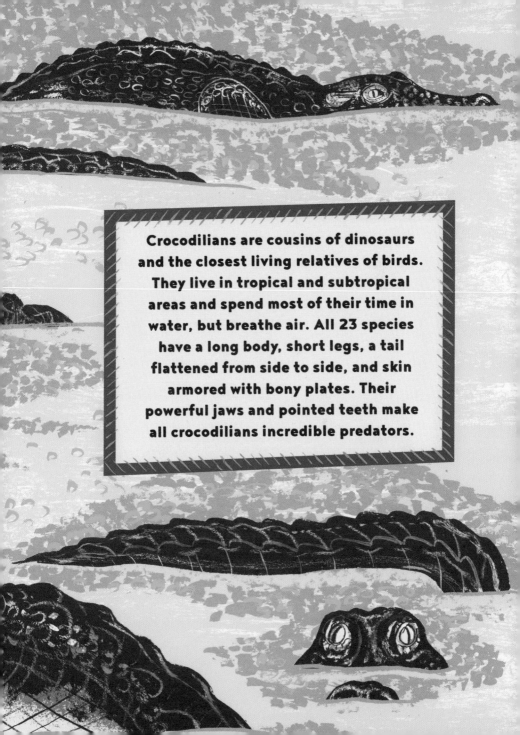

Crocodilians are cousins of dinosaurs and the closest living relatives of birds. They live in tropical and subtropical areas and spend most of their time in water, but breathe air. All 23 species have a long body, short legs, a tail flattened from side to side, and skin armored with bony plates. Their powerful jaws and pointed teeth make all crocodilians incredible predators.

CROCODILES

family name	number of species
Crocodylidae	**14**

Crocodiles differ from alligators. They have a V–shaped snout and teeth that poke out when their mouth is shut. All crocodilians are powerful swimmers and are able to leap from water with spectacular speed when attacking, using their tail for propulsion. On land they can gallop short distances but, contrary to popular myth, not fast enough to catch a running human.

Saltwater crocodile

EXAMPLE: SALTWATER CROCODILE *(Crocodylus porosus)*

SEAGOING GIANT

Saltwater crocodiles are the world's largest living reptiles. They live in rivers, marshes, and estuaries close to the ocean, occasionally swimming far out to sea and traveling hundreds of miles with the aid of ocean currents. Their huge size makes them a threat to many other animals sharing the water, including fish (even sharks!), birds, mammals, and humans.

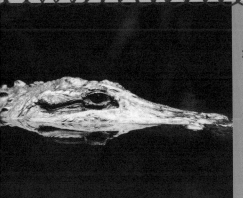

A CLOSER LOOK

» LIFESPAN
Up to 70 years in the wild, 100 in captivity

» SIZE
Males up to 20 ft long, females half this size

» WEIGHT
Males up to 2,500 lb

» DIET
Fish, birds, mammals, other reptiles; prey size increases with growth

» CONSERVATION STATUS
Extinct in parts of range, but doing well in areas where it is protected.

» LOCATION
Southern India, Bangladesh, Sri Lanka, parts of Indonesia, New Guinea, Philippines, and Australia

DID YOU KNOW?

* Crocodiles are quite vocal. Adults make growling and hissing sounds and babies call from their eggs when they are ready to hatch.

* The largest saltwater crocodiles may have measured 23 feet long and weighed 4,500 lb, but no crocodile this large has been seen recently.

* A crocodile brain is tiny! It is between 0.1 and 0.05% the weight of its body. A human brain is about 2% of our bodyweight.

* A saltwater crocodile can bite with a force of 16,400 Newtons, about 25 times harder than an average human. Snap!

Narrow snout

Interlocking teeth

ALLIGATORS & CAIMANS

family name	number of species
Alligatoridae	**8**

This group includes two species of alligator and six caimans, ranging in size from Cuvier's dwarf caiman (5 feet) to the American alligator (sometimes over 15 feet). All but the Chinese alligator live in the Americas, spending much of their time in water. They emerge to warm their ectothermic bodies in the sun, often in large groups. Caimans differ slightly from alligators in the structure of the nose and the arrangement of bony plates in their skin.

American alligator

WETLAND ARCHITECT

The American alligator has few natural predators, but 50 years ago it become rare due to hunting by people. The species has now been protected for 50 years and has increased to healthy numbers. It is the top predator in the swamps and rivers where it lives, but also creates a habitat for other wildlife by digging pools called "gator holes" where it wallows in very hot weather.

A CLOSER LOOK

» LIFESPAN
Up to 50 years

» SIZE
Up to 20 ft long

» WEIGHT
Up to 1,000 lb

» DIET
Fish, turtles, birds, small- to medium-sized mammals, insects, and, occasionally, people

» CONSERVATION STATUS
Population may now exceed 5 million thanks to conservation

» LOCATION
Southeastern USA

DID YOU KNOW?

★ Alligators and other large crocodilians can survive three years without food, relying on a low-energy lifestyle to conserve their reserves.

★ Alligator teeth are replaced as they wear out and an animal can grow 3,000 teeth in a lifetime.

★ Some of the mating calls used by male alligators are too low-pitched for humans to hear.

★ American alligator eggs incubated at 90°F tend to be male, but warmer or cooler temperatures produce mostly females.

U-shaped snout

SNAKES

Snakes are legless, scaly predators, found on all continents except Antarctica. Most snakes have a single row of wide scales running down their belly. Their flexible jaws can separate sideways to swallow prey much larger than their own head. Snakes have no visible ears, but are very sensitive to vibrations and chemicals in the air. They regularly shed their scaly skins as they grow.

VIPERS

family name	number of species
Viperidae	**224**

Vipers are a group of snakes that disable prey by injecting venom through their hollow fangs. This venom is slower-acting than toxins used by some other snakes, so after a bite, the snake must track its victim using super-sharp senses of taste and smell. Vipers range in size from the 8-inch Namaqua dwarf adder, to bushmasters and rattlesnakes ten times as long! Most vipers give birth to live young.

Fang

Eastern diamond-back
rattlesnake

EXAMPLE: EASTERN DIAMONDBACK RATTLESNAKE *(Crotalus adamanteus)*

AMERICAN HEAVYWEIGHT

This magnificent reptile is among the largest venomous snakes. It belongs to a group known as pit vipers, after the small holes between the eye and nostril on each side. These pits can detect tiny amounts of infrared heat. The diamondback's venom not only disables prey, it also marks it—the snake can follow the distinctive chemical trail left by an animal it has bitten.

Tail

A CLOSER LOOK

» LIFESPAN
Up to 20 years

» SIZE
Up to 8 ft

» WEIGHT
Up to 34 lb

» DIET
Small mammals and birds. Large individuals can take tigers, panthers, and crocodiles

» CONSERVATION STATUS
Declining, but not yet considered endangered

» LOCATION
Southeastern USA

DID YOU KNOW?

★ Rattlesnake tail muscles vibrate up to 50 times a second, creating a noisy warning to other animals that might attack.

★ Rattlesnake fangs fold away when not in use.

★ Not all rattlesnake bites inject venom. If you're lucky it'll be a warning "dry bite."

★ Because rattlesnake venom attacks living cells, it starts the process of breaking down cells before the meal is even swallowed.

BOAS

family name	number of species
Boidae	**49**

Boas are medium to large snakes that are closely related to pythons. All modern species coil their body tightly around prey until it becomes unable to breathe, a process known as constriction. They can easily kill prey larger than themselves, and swallow it whole. These very large meals can take weeks to digest. Unlike pythons, boas give birth to live young. Young boas spend most of their time in trees but become less agile climbers as they grow.

Green anaconda

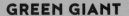 
GREEN GIANT

The green anaconda may not be the world's longest snake, but it is the heaviest. Its massive muscular coils can subdue prey as large as tapirs and pig-like peccaries. The species is an excellent swimmer and lives in swamps and forests of the Amazon and Orinoco rivers. Much of its prey is ambushed from the murky water.

DID YOU KNOW?

★ A boa holds its victims so tightly that they cannot breathe.

★ There are reports of green anacondas over 40 feet long, but these have been disputed. Live snakes are very difficult to measure accurately.

★ Anaconda babies are left to look after themselves as soon as they are born.

★ Anacondas often lie in the shallows and hunt their prey by ambushing them.

A CLOSER LOOK

» **LIFESPAN**
Up to 30 years

» **SIZE**
Occasionally over 20 ft

» **WEIGHT**
Up to 550 lb

» **DIET**
Small- and medium-sized mammals, birds, fish, and reptiles, including other anacondas

» **CONSERVATION STATUS**
Not well known, but likely to be declining due to hunting and habitat loss

» **LOCATION**
Northern South America

PYTHONS

family name	number of species
Pythonidae	**31**

Pythons live in Africa, Asia, and Australia and they have been introduced to Florida in the USA. Like boas, they are ambush predators that kill by constriction, first snagging their prey with sharp, backward-curving teeth, then wrapping around it until it dies. Large pythons have occasionally been known to kill humans and swallow them whole. Females lay clutches of up to a few dozen eggs and incubate them until they hatch.

Reticulated python

LONG STORY

The reticulated python is the world's longest snake, however many accounts of pythons over 30 feet are exaggerations or measurements taken from stretched skins. It lives in forests and grasslands, often close to water. Its body is patterned in bronze and black with paler lines of white or gold that break up its outline and make it difficult to spot in shadowy vegetation.

A CLOSER LOOK

» LIFESPAN
15-30 years

» SIZE
Up to and over 25 ft

» WEIGHT
Sometimes over 320 lb

» DIET
Small- to medium-sized mammals

» CONSERVATION STATUS
Not threatened

» LOCATION
Southeast Asia, Western Bangladesh, Vietnam, USA

DID YOU KNOW?

★ Pythons will tackle prey up to and over their own body weight, and up to a quarter of their own length.

★ The elasticated jaws of a python separate, allowing it to swallow huge meals in one go.

★ As well as basking, pythons can shiver to generate heat for themselves and to warm their eggs.

★ Pythons are often found close to water, and have reached islands by swimming many miles.

TYPICAL SNAKES

family name	number of species
Colubridae	**1938**

This huge group contains two-thirds of all snake species, and it is a bit of a mixed bag. In fact, some so-called colubrids may belong in different groups, but scientists still need to carry out further tests to work out how they are related. Colubrids live on all continents except Antarctica. They are mostly egg layers and are generally considered only mildly or non-venomous, with a few exceptions such as the boomslang snake.

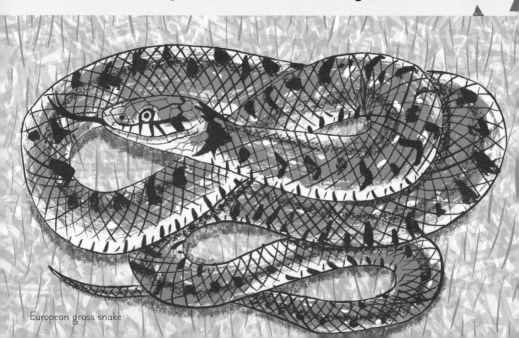

European grass snake

NORTHERN STAR

The grass snake is a widespread species and one of the most northerly dwelling reptiles. It lives in burrows to avoid freezing temperatures and hibernates in winter when food is scarce. It is an excellent swimmer, able to dive for up to 30 minutes at a time, and most of its food is caught in the water.

A CLOSER LOOK

» **LIFESPAN**
15-25 years

» **SIZE**
Females up to 4 ft long, males smaller

» **WEIGHT**
Up to 0.5 lb

» **DIET**
Frogs and toads

» **CONSERVATION STATUS**
Relatively common and widespread; up to 320,000 in UK alone

» **LOCATION**
Europe and North Africa

DID YOU KNOW?

★ Grass snakes in cool climates use the heat generated by rotting vegetation to incubate their eggs.

★ The scientific name *Natrix* comes from the Latin *natare* meaning "to swim."

★ The grass snake is one of very few reptiles able to live north of the Arctic Circle.

★ Trapped grass snakes often release a disgusting smell to deter predators from eating them.

★ When cornered, a grass snake plays dead.

Playing dead

COBRAS

family name	number of species
Elapidae	**37**

The elapids are a group of highly venomous snakes including cobras, mambas, and sea snakes. Their venom works on the victim's nervous system and is very fast acting. It is used to paralyze and kill prey, and also in self-defense. Spitting cobras are able to squirt venom several yards, usually aiming for the eyes of an attacker. Rearing and swaying helps the snake target a strike. When it comes in contact with skin or eyes, the venom causes a burning sensation and can lead to blindness.

King cobra

THE SNAKE EATER

The king cobra specializes in hunting other snakes. It is large, fast, and agile, with excellent eyesight, and can track its prey by smell from several hundred yards away. If injected, its venom can kill a person in 30 minutes. Even elephants have been known to die from king cobra bites. The king cobra only needs to make one kill a month to survive.

A CLOSER LOOK

» LIFESPAN
Up to 25 years

» SIZE
Up to 18 ft

» WEIGHT
Up to 25 lb

» DIET
Small mammals, lizards, birds, and other snakes

» CONSERVATION STATUS
Vulnerable to extinction due to habitat loss and hunting

» LOCATION
India, southern China, and Southeast Asia

DID YOU KNOW?

* All cobras can be deadly to humans, but one-third of strikes are "dry bites" with no venom injected.

* One way to try and escape an angry cobra is to throw down a hat or item of clothing to distract it, while backing away.

* Female king cobras guard their eggs carefully until just before hatching, then leave to avoid the urge to eat their own babies!

* Cobras are surprisingly noisy, producing a variety of growling and hissing sounds.

Like other cobras, the king can raise the front third of its body off the ground and flatten its neck to appear bigger than it really is.

BLIND SNAKES

Infraorder name	number of species
Scolecophidia	**440**

The blind snakes include five families of mainly small, burrowing snakes found in tropical forests. Blind snake bodies are covered in tiny scales, giving them a very smooth surface that slips easily through soil and leaf litter. Eyesight is little use in total darkness, and the tiny eyes of blind snakes do no more than tell light from dark. Blind snakes hunt small invertebrates, which they track by scent.

Barbados threadsnake

SPAGHETTI SNAKE

This incredible creature, discovered in 2008, is the smallest-known snake species. Adults are no thicker than a cooked strand of spaghetti. Any smaller, and scientists think the young would not be able to find prey tiny enough. Females lay just one long narrow egg at a time, containing a single baby roughly half their own length.

A CLOSER LOOK

» **LIFESPAN**
Unknown

» **SIZE**
Up to 4 in

» **WEIGHT**
Less than 1 g

» **DIET**
Ants and termites

» **CONSERVATION STATUS**
Critically endangered due to loss of forest habitat

» **LOCATION**
Barbados

DID YOU KNOW?

★ The Barbados threadsnake can easily curl up on a quarter.

★ The entire population of Barbados threadsnakes lives in a tiny area of forest covering less than 4 square miles.

★ Blind snakes in general use potent chemicals to protect themselves from attack by angry ants and termites.

★ Several species of threadsnake are able to reproduce without mating.

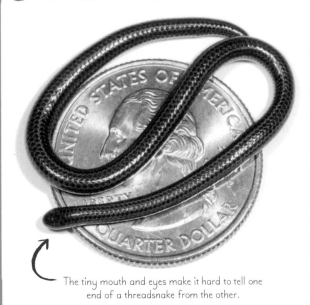

The tiny mouth and eyes make it hard to tell one end of a threadsnake from the other.

LIZARDS

Lizards are hugely successful reptiles, found in many habitats from deserts and forests, to mountains and oceanic islands. Most have four legs, but several hundred species are legless. Lizards typically have scaly or bumpy skin, which they shed in patches as they grow. Many lizards can shed their tail if they are caught by it so they can escape.

CHAMELEONS

family name	number of species
Chamaeleonidae	**202**

These unmistakeable Old World lizards have grasping feet and tails, long elastic tongues, and eyes that move independently to give 360° vision. They can display a variety of skin patterns and colors. This color-changing power helps them to camouflage and communicate. Bright colors indicate aggression or excitement; dark ones suggest stress or submission. They change color by varying the arrangement of pigments and light-reflecting crystals in their skin cells.

Panther
chameleon

KALEIDOSCOPIC COLOR

Panther chameleons are native to Madagascar, where they occupy dry open forests. They are surprisingly short-lived for their size, developing rapidly after hatching, breeding as young as six months but often living only a year in the wild.

Females are typically colored pink or green, but males develop a stunning range of patterns and colors including green, blue, turquoise, pink, orange, yellow, and red. The colors are brightest during courtship.

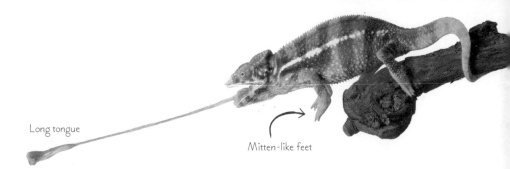

Long tongue

Mitten-like feet

DID YOU KNOW?

★ The name chameleon comes from the Greek *khamailéōn*, meaning "ground lion."

★ A chameleon tongue-strike is faster than the human eye can see. Victims have less than a tenth of a second to escape.

★ More than half of all chameleon species are native to Madagascar, a huge island isolated from the rest of Africa for around 88 million years.

★ Some chameleons change color to avoid particular types of predator, for example choosing colors certain birds or snakes find harder to see.

A CLOSER LOOK

» LIFESPAN
1-3 years

» SIZE
10-20 in long, including tail (females smaller than males)

» WEIGHT
Up to 0.4 lb

» DIET
Small prey, mostly invertebrates, and some plant material

» CONSERVATION STATUS
Stable

» LOCATION
Madagascar, introduced to the islands of Réunion and Mauritius

GECKOS

family name	number of species
Gekkonidae	**950**

Geckos are the most species-rich family of lizards. Their colorful skin is covered in small granular bumps instead of scales. Most species have sticky toe pads made up of microscopic, closely packed hairs, allowing them to climb vertical or overhanging surfaces as smooth as glass. The tails of geckos are fragile and can be dropped if attacked In some species the tail is head-shaped to distract predators from the real head.

Tokay gecko

THE LIZARD THAT SHOUTS ITS NAME

This large, colorful gecko is a naturally widespread, nocturnal lizard found in tropical forests. It also regularly enters houses, where it is usually welcome as an eager predator of pests such as cockroaches, mosquitoes, and even baby mice. Like many geckos, the tokay is territorial and very noisy for a reptile, calling at night to attract mates and warn off rivals. The words "gecko" and "tokay" both come from the chirping call of the male, which sounds like "gek-ko...gek-ko..."

Large eyes

DID YOU KNOW?

★ The hairs on a gecko's feet are so tiny that, in some species, more than 14,000 cluster in a square millimeter.

★ Gecko toes flex in both directions, making them appear double jointed. This helps a gecko peel its sticky feet from surfaces as it climbs.

★ Many geckos lack eyelids and use their tongue to wipe their eyes clean.

★ The largest-known gecko was the New Zealand *kawekaweau*, which is sadly now extinct. It is known only from a museum specimen 2 feet long.

A CLOSER LOOK

» LIFESPAN
Up to 10 years in the wild

» SIZE
Males up to 16 in long including tail, females up to 11 in

» WEIGHT
Up to 0.7 lb

» DIET
Mainly insects and other invertebrates, occasionally small birds, frogs, or mammals

» CONSERVATION STATUS
Widespread and relatively common

» LOCATION
Southern Asia, from India to Indonesia and the Philippines

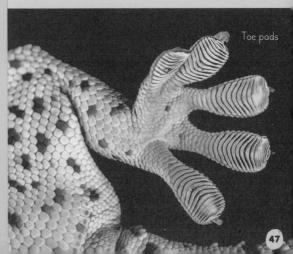

Toe pads

IGUANAS

family name	number of species
Iguanidae	**35**

This small group of handsome lizards is adapted to tough, often dry habitats. They are found in dry forests, savannas, and rocky habitats of the Americas, Antilles, and certain Pacific islands including Fiji and Galápagos. The green iguana is the biggest, at 6 feet, but they range in size. As adults, they are wholly vegetarian, eating mainly leaves and fruit, though youngsters may eat insects or other small invertebrates. All iguana species are egg-layers, using burrows or crevices as nests.

Marine iguana

DARWIN'S DRAGONS

Marine iguanas are the only lizards dependent on the ocean. They live on the Galápagos Islands, along with three land-dwelling species. The islands are volcanic, with little vegetation, so the marine iguanas have adapted to eat seaweed. They dive up to 80 feet in the cold seas surrounding the islands. On land they have to spend most of their time basking to warm their bodies. They sleep and bask in groups to protect themselves from predators.

DID YOU KNOW?

★ The ancestors of marine iguanas probably floated to the Galápagos islands on natural rafts from South America about 10 million years ago.

★ Marine iguanas are very sluggish when cold, and rely on aggression to deter possible predators, rather than running away.

★ Excess salt from food and seawater is removed from the marine iguana's blood by a gland in the nostrils, and sneezed out as super-salty snot.

★ Breeding male marine iguanas are highly territorial and fighting is very common. The dominant males develop striking red and green colors.

A CLOSER LOOK

» LIFESPAN
Up to 12 years

» SIZE
Varies: 1-4 ft long
including tail

» WEIGHT
Up to 26 lb

» DIET
Marine algae
(seaweed) only

» CONSERVATION STATUS
Vulnerable to extinction due to limited habitats, predation, and climate change

» LOCATION
Galápagos Islands only

Black, heat-absorbing skin

MONITOR LIZARDS

family name	number of species
Varanidae	**50–60**

These impressive lizards range in size from 8 inches to 10 feet in total length. All have small round scales like chain mail, arranged in rings around the body. Many species are able to stand up on two legs, supported by the tail, to "monitor" their surroundings. All species are active predators. Monitors show unusual levels of intelligence and personality for reptiles. Experiments suggest some can count up to six, and Komodo dragons appear to use teamwork when hunting.

Komodo dragon

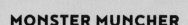
MONSTER MUNCHER

The world's largest lizard is the top predator on a scatter of Indonesian islands, tackling prey as large as water buffalo. These creatures were once thought to kill prey with a filthy bacteria-infected bite. In truth, most probably die of shock and blood loss, possibly aided by a variety of toxins that mix with the Komodo's saliva. The dragon rips chunks from its prey or swallows it whole, and after a large meal may not eat again for another month.

orked tongue

DID YOU KNOW?

★ The giant goanna, a monitor lizard twice as big as the Komodo dragon, lived in Australia until about 50,000 years ago. It was probably hunted to extinction by early human settlers.

★ Komodo dragons produce copious saliva, which is often pink as their gums bleed easily.

★ Komodo dragons owe part of their speed and stamina to a heart built more like that of a mammal than a standard reptile.

★ Komodo dragons have limited hearing and poor eyesight but can scent prey from over 5 miles away.

A CLOSER LOOK

» LIFESPAN
Up to 30 years

» SIZE
Up to 10 ft long, including tail

» WEIGHT
Up to 360 lb, though 150 lb is more normal

» DIET
Hunts medium to large prey, including young of own species; often scavenges

» CONSERVATION STATUS
Vulnerable and declining; wild population about 3,000

» LOCATION
A few smaller Indonesian islands, including Komodo and Rinca

WALL LIZARDS

family name	number of species
Lacertidae	**300+**

The wall lizards are small- to medium-sized Old World lizards with slim bodies and long tails, which they are able to drop if attacked. They typically occupy grasslands, moorlands, and scrub and occur up to 10,000 feet above sea level, much higher than other groups. Most are highly active, agile predators of insects and other invertebrates, which are snapped up and swallowed whole. A wide variety of breeding strategies helps makes this a very successful group.

Common lizard

WORLD'S BEST REPTILE?

The common lizard occupies a bigger habitat range than any other reptile. The species shows extreme variability in lifestyle, with those that give birth to live young thriving in the frozen north, even within the Arctic Circle, and egg-layers in the south. It climbs and swims well, and can move extremely fast once warmed to its ideal body temperature of 86° Fahrenheit, by basking in the sun.

Scales

DID YOU KNOW?

★ The common lizard is the only reptile native to Ireland.

★ In parts of its range where winters are cold, common lizards hibernate. In the warmer southern range, the species remains active all year.

★ Live-bearing common lizards do not interbreed with egg-laying ones. The two types are on their way to becoming different species.

★ Female common lizards either produce a few large young or many small young. Overall, this allows the species to thrive in a wider variety of circumstances.

A CLOSER LOOK

» LIFESPAN
Up to 8 years

» SIZE
Up to 8 in long (including up to 6 in of tail)

» WEIGHT
Up to 10 g

» DIET
Invertebrates including insects, spiders, small slugs, and worms

» CONSERVATION STATUS
Common and widespread

» LOCATION
Europe and northern temperate Asia, from the British Isles to China and Japan

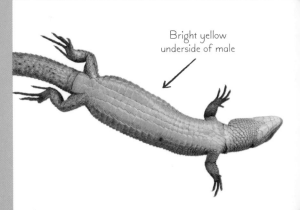

Bright yellow underside of male

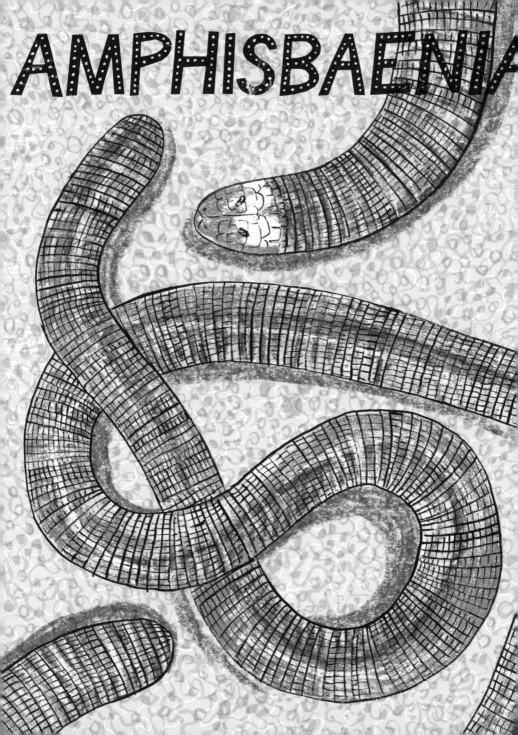

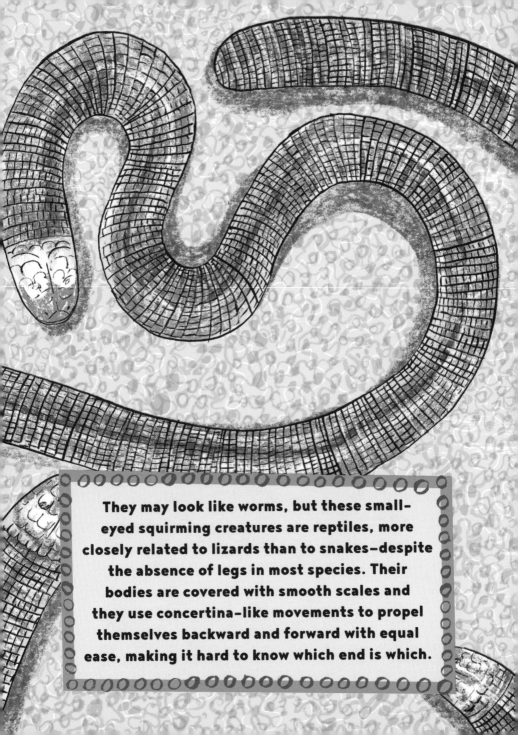

They may look like worms, but these small-eyed squirming creatures are reptiles, more closely related to lizards than to snakes—despite the absence of legs in most species. Their bodies are covered with smooth scales and they use concertina-like movements to propel themselves backward and forward with equal ease, making it hard to know which end is which.

WORM LIZARD

family name	number of species
Amphisbaenidae	**180**

Amphisbaenians are legless burrowing lizards that spend their entire lives underground. They resemble very large, powerful earthworms, with reduced eyes and ears, and a ringed body. However, their scales and flickering forked tongue make it clear they are reptiles and their behavior is not at all wormlike. They are active predators, tracking down prey using scent and vibration before delivering powerful bites with large back-curved teeth.

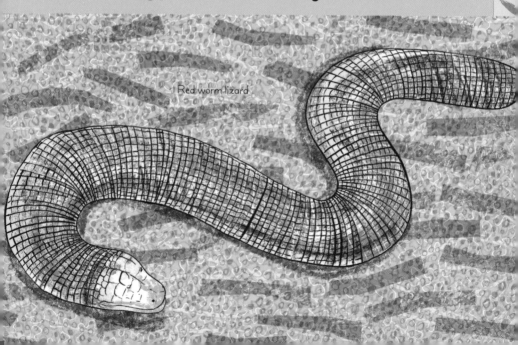

Red worm lizard

EXAMPLE: RED WORM LIZARD *(Amphisbaena alba)*

LEGLESS WONDER

This large and widespread worm lizard, found in forest and grassland habitats, is often associated with ant and termite nests. Females lay eggs inside the nests so hatchlings have an easy source of food. The red worm lizard is a powerful burrower, and uses its blunt head to force its way though soil and leaf litter. The bones of the skull are fused for extra strength. It also swims well.

A CLOSER LOOK

» LIFESPAN
Unknown

» SIZE
Up to 30 in long

» WEIGHT
Up to 0.5 lb

» DIET
Small animal prey found underground including: insects, spiders, and baby mice. Also some plant material

» CONSERVATION STATUS
Population unknown

» LOCATION
South America, from Venezuela to northern Argentina, also the Antilles, Trinidad and Tobago

DID YOU KNOW?

★ Worm lizards evolved in North America. The ancestors of European and African species must have crossed the Atlantic Ocean by swimming or rafting on masses of soil bound up by the roots of floating trees.

★ Four species of worm lizard in the genus *Bipes* have retained one pair of legs, at the front.

★ Amphisbaenians are named after a mythical Greek serpent, *Amphisbaena*, which supposedly had a head at each end.

★ When threatened, a worm lizard curves its body around and raises both its head and tail. It is difficult for an attacker to know which end is which.

Scales arranged in rings

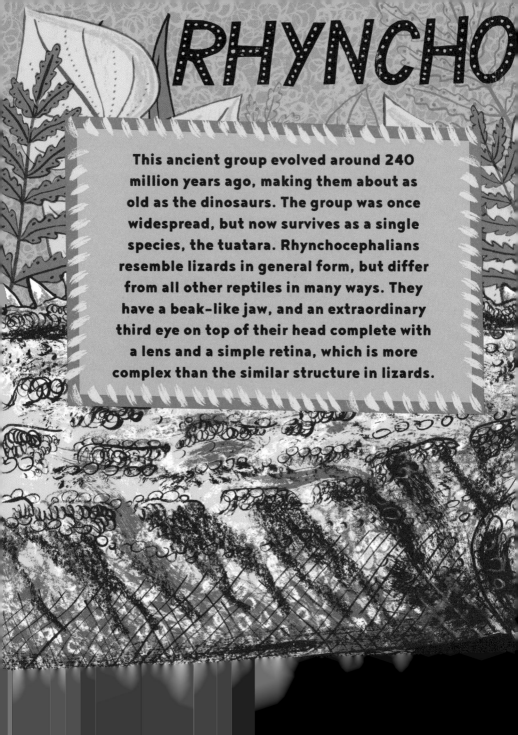

This ancient group evolved around 240 million years ago, making them about as old as the dinosaurs. The group was once widespread, but now survives as a single species, the tuatara. Rhynchocephalians resemble lizards in general form, but differ from all other reptiles in many ways. They have a beak-like jaw, and an extraordinary third eye on top of their head complete with a lens and a simple retina, which is more complex than the similar structure in lizards.

TUATARA

family name
Sphenodontidae

number of species
1

New Zealand is the only place where these extraordinary reptiles survive. Tuataras are ground-dwelling, largely nocturnal animals that survive by living an exceptionally slow lifestyle. They hibernate in winter, but even when awake only breathe about five times and have seven heartbeats a minute. Tuataras are cool-bodied, and are able to function at temperatures as low as 41° Fahrenheit—the lowest operational body temperature of any reptile.

Northern tuatara

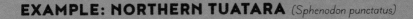

CONSERVATION

Now the only recognized species of its kind, the northern tuatara was driven extinct on the mainland of New Zealand by introduced predators, in particular rats, which easily kill eggs and hatchlings. For more than 200 years, tuataras lived only on offshore islands, but thanks to intensive conservation, numbers are increasing. There is a successful captive breeding program, and in 2009 young were once again hatched in the wild on the mainland, in a sanctuary surrounded by rat-proof fencing.

A CLOSER LOOK

» LIFESPAN
120 years or more

» SIZE
Up to 30 in long including tail

» WEIGHT
Up to 3 lb

» DIET
Invertebrates such as crickets, beetles, spiders, and small vertebrates including frogs, bird eggs, and chicks

» CONSERVATION STATUS
Population 60,000–100,000, highly protected and responding to conservation

» LOCATION
New Zealand only, mainly restricted to offshore islands

DID YOU KNOW?

★ Tuatara teeth are spiky projections of their jawbones, which wear down as they age. Two upper tooth rows of teeth interlock with one row in the lower jaw, and the bite is severe.

★ Tuatara eggs incubated above 70° Fahrenheit will be male. Below 70° they will be female. Incubation at precisely 70° produces a mixed brood of males and females.

★ In 2009, in New Zealand's Southland Museum, 11 healthy baby tuatara hatched from eggs laid by an 80-year-old female and fathered by a 111-year-old male.

★ Tuataras bask to raise their body temperature on cool mornings, but not too high. For them, a body temperature of over 82° Fahrenheit is fatal.

Photographic acknowledgments: p.37 Grass snake feigning death © Alamy Stock Photo; p.41
Barbados Threadsnake © S. Blair Hedges. p.57 Giant Amphisbaena © Alamy Stock Photo; p.61
Tuatara © Alamy Stock Photo; All other photographs © Shutterstock.

Brimming with creative inspiration, how-to projects, and useful
information to enrich your everyday life, Quarto Knows is a favorite
destination for those pursuing their interests and passions. Visit our
site and dig deeper with our books into your area of interest:
Quarto Creates, Quarto Cooks, Quarto Homes, Quarto Lives,
Quarto Drives, Quarto Explores, Quarto Gifts, or Quarto Kids.

Pocket Guide to Turtles, Snakes, and Other Reptiles © 2018 Quarto Publishing plc.
Text written by Amy-Jane Beer. Illustrations © 2018 Alice Pattullo.

First Published in 2018 by Lincoln Children's Books,
an imprint of The Quarto Group.
400 First Avenue North, Suite 400, Minneapolis, MN 55401, USA.
T (612) 344-8100 F (612) 344-8692 **www.QuartoKnows.com**

The right of Alice Pattullo to be identified as the illustrator and Amy-Jane Beer to be identified as the author of
this work has been asserted by them in accordance with the Copyright, Designs and Patents Act, 1988 (United
Kingdom).

Published in association with the Natural History Museum, London.

ISBN 978-1-78603-112-9

Illustrated with brush and Indian ink, collaged hand-painted patterns, and digital composition.
Set in Pistacho Soft, Noyh A Bistro, and handlettered text

Published by Rachel Williams and Jenny Broom
Designed by Nicola Price
Edited by Katy Flint
Production by Jenny Cundill

Manufactured in Dongguan, China in TL052018

9 8 7 6 5 4 3 2 1